Joey's Monkey

By Cameron Macintosh

T0360148

Joey loved Pete,
his fluffy monkey.

But today, when Joey sat up
in bed, Pete was missing!

Joey did a big leap off his bed.

He went to look for his monkey.

Joey looked on the seat,
but Pete was not there.

Joey peeked up the chimney,
but no Pete!

Joey checked out on
the concrete.

Pete was not there, but ...

Joey **could** see Pete.

The monkey was up in a tree!

Bea the cat was up
in the tree, too.

Bea looked down at Joey.

"Bea!" yelled Joey.
"Did you drag Pete up
into that tree?"

"Here is a deal, Bea,"
said Joey.
"I will hand you a treat,
and you bring Pete down."

Bea got the treat, but then she went back up ... and up!

Pete was **still** in the tree!

"You are so mean, Bea!"
said Joey.

Joey got a hockey stick
and gave Pete a tap.

Pete fell down in a heap.

Joey got Pete and
squeezed him!

CHECKING FOR MEANING

1. Where does Joey look for Pete? *(Literal)*

2. How did Pete get up in the tree? *(Literal)*

3. Why did Joey squeeze Pete when he got him down from the tree? *(Inferential)*

EXTENDING VOCABULARY

peeked	What does *peeked* mean? When have you peeked at something? What did you see? Is a peek a quick look or a longer, slower look?
treat	What is a *treat*? Is it something you have all the time, or only on a special occasion? What treats do you like? What treat would Joey have given Bea?
squeezed	What is another word with a similar meaning to *squeezed* that could have been used in the story? E.g. hugged, cuddled, held.

MOVING BEYOND THE TEXT

1. Why do lots of children take a special toy to bed?

2. What was Joey's deal with Bea? Have you ever made a deal with someone? What was it? Was it successful?

3. Can you think of another method Joey could have used to get Pete out of the tree?

4. What could Joey do to stop Bea taking Pete again?

SPELLINGS FOR THE LONG /e/ VOWEL SOUND

| e | ee | ie | ea | e_e | y | ey |

PRACTICE WORDS

Joey

Pete

fluffy

monkey

seat

peeked

chimney

concrete

see

tree

Bea

deal

treat

mean

hockey

heap

squeezed

leap